Blenheim

by D. S. V. Fosten with artwork by B. K. Fosten

ALMARK

ALMARK PUBLISHING CO. LTD., LONDON

First published 1975

ISBN 85524 220 5 (paper cover)
ISBN 85524 221 3 (hard cover)

Printed in Great Britain by
Pan Litho Ltd.,
Pan House,
172-176 The Highway,
London E19DD.
for the publishers, Almark Publishing Co. Ltd.,
49 Malden Way, New Malden,
Surrey KT3 EA, England.

Contents

Foreword

The decisive victory of Blenheim was said by Allison to "resound through every part of Europe". It was the first substantial victory over a French Army which had been considered as invincible since its re-organisation by Louvois in the 17th Century.

Skilfully engineered by the Duke of Marlborough and the Savoyard Prince Eugene it resulted in the virtual destruction of a powerful Franco-Bavarian Army under the command of two of Louis XIV's most experienced marshals and saved Austria from almost certain defeat and occupation. In writing this short account of the magnificent march and the subsequent campaign in the valley of the Danube I have to acknowledge my debt to David Chandler and his definitive works "A Travellers Guide to the Battlefields of Europe" and "Marlborough as Military Commander". Major R. E. Scouller's excellent "The Armies of Queen Anne" is the proper reference material for any student of the economy of the British Army of the period and for general information on the Marlburian campaigns as a whole I recommend Frank Taylor's "The Wars of Marlborough", which is in two volumes, and Sir G. M. Trevelyan's major history "England in the Reign of Queen Anne", which is in three volumes.

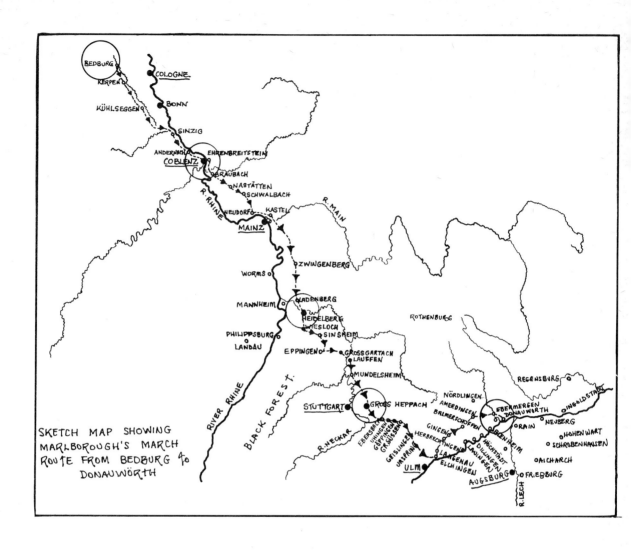

SKETCH MAP SHOWING MARLBOROUGH'S MARCH ROUTE FROM BEDBURG to DONAUWÖRTH

Introduction

Charles II, King of Spain was an impotent imbecile and a dying man. As the 17th century drew to a close, three major claimants to his throne were manoeuvring for position under the patronage of the great rulers of Europe, Louis XIV of France, Leopold I of Austria and William III of Holland and Great Britain. These claimants were the Bourbon Prince Phillipe, the Hapsburg Archduke Leopold and Joseph Ferdinand of Bavaria. Joseph Ferdinand narrowed the field by dying in February 1699, twenty months before Charles. Under the Partition Treaties, which had been so adroitly engineered by William of Orange, Louis XIV had reluctantly agreed to renounce all the claims of his family to the Spanish throne. However, before Charles eventually died, in November 1700, he made a new will leaving the throne to Louis' grandson. At first the French king showed a reluctance to accept this turn of events but he soon publicly acknowledged Phillipe d'Anjou as the Spanish King. He was shortly to set the seal on England's antagonism when he further announced his support for the claim to the English throne of James Stuart and, even more conducive to British anger, the reinstatement of the Roman Catholic Church.

As a result of these events England, the Holy Roman Empire and the United Provinces of Holland formed a coalition against Louis XIV. This treaty, called the "Treaty of Alliance" was signed in 1701.

Whilst negotiating this tenuous alliance with Antoine Heinsius, the Grand Pensionary of Holland, King William was killed in a hunting accident and the last of the Stuarts, Queen Anne, ascended the British throne.

On 15th May 1702, England declared war on France and Spain who had formed their countries into a rival coalition called the "Alliance of the two Crowns".

No sooner had Louis publicly declared his grandson as King of Spain than large French armies moved into the Spanish Netherlands and occupied the fortresses along the borders, including Namur and Liege.

From 1701 to 1704 the fortunes of war alternated between France and the Coalition. Marlborough set siege to and captured some fortresses and the French, under Marshal de Villars, gained a notable victory at Höchstädt near Blenheim. Marshal de Tallard beat an Imperial (Austrian) army near Spiers and regained the fortress of Landau for France. A large Franco-Bavarian army had massed in the Danubian valley with further forces in Northern Italy and de Tallard had another large army near the Rhine.

Encouraged by the negative approach of the stolid Dutch generals the French began preparations to move on the Imperial capital, Vienna. The Imperial forces in the area were not strong enough to withstand such an attack especially as they were being hard pressed by Hungarian national revolutionaries under Count Racoczi on their eastern borders. For Louis XIV, 1704 opened with great prospects. The Netherlands were so closely planted with fortresses as to render decisive victories unlikely in that area nor could any limited field successes help the Coalition to save Vienna. The unimaginative Dutch generals, always cautious and loath to use their mainly mercenary armies in any scheme which had uncertain benefits, could see no way out of the situation.

Marlborough saw that the only practical solution was to defeat the great French army in the field and preferably in the Danube area. He therefore conceived, and secretly negotiated, the brilliant strategy of marching south with part of the Anglo-Dutch army, drawing off the French threat to Vienna, and bringing them to battle. Because he realised that the Dutch leaders would almost certainly refuse permission for such a revolutionary and daring scheme, he was forced to plan his campaign in complete secrecy and to mask his real intentions from his allies.

The plan was dangerous. It would mean that to march, even to the Rhine, Marlborough would have to move over open ground across the face of two French armies under Marshals de Villars and de Coignies and take a large force, at speed, through nearly 300 miles of unfamiliar and difficult country. The possible wastage of men and equipment would be devastating.

He pretended to the Dutch that he was going to operate only in the Moselle Valley but so many objections were raised even to this limited scheme that he had to threaten to withdraw his British contingent and to march alone. As a concession he undertook to leave General Overkirk in Holland with a part of the army to defend the Low Countries against any French surprise attack.

It was on the 20th May 1704 that Marlborough began a course of action which was unparalleled at that time. It took all the devious ingenuity of the Duke and his Quartermaster-General, William Cadogan, to get the army ready for the great march without revealing his true intentions to the Dutch States-General.

Before the march was started, Cadogan had the task of assembling the vast numbers of waggons and carts of all types to carry the ammunition, baggage and provisions. Five thousand horses had to be found together with sufficient peasant carters and waggoners to conduct the great column. Because time was so short, Marlborough decided to travel as light as possible and decided to send the heavier equipment and stores down the Rhine by barges. He also decided to leave much of the siege artillery behind, assuming that he would be able to find sufficient heavy guns in south Germany as substitutes.

1 The March to the Danube

Twenty one thousand men started the march, crossing the River Maas by a hastily constructed pontoon bridge near Ruremonde and making rendezvous at Bedburg with about 2000 waggons and carts.

The roads of Europe in the eighteenth century were atrocious by modern standards. Earth bound, they were pitted and rutted by the constant movement of waggons, horses and cattle and were almost impassable in inclement weather.

From the outset Marlborough was beset by foul weather. The early summer of 1704 was very wet and the marching column found the roads as bad as they could be. The cavalry marched due south, ahead of the main column, through the small towns of Kerpen, Kühlseggen and Andernach, followed by the great bulk of the horse-drawn transport and the artillery train; the remainder of the baggage bringing up the rear. To avoid the laborious task of picking their way through the deep muddy ruts made by the wheeled transport, the marching men were strung out along the flanks and marched on the verges, or even outside the great ditches which flanked the highways. Outside the main stream of the columns and acting as a protective screen of scouts rode the dragoons. Marlborough started the march with thirty four field pieces and four howitzers but was to pick up additional guns on the way.

The infantry carried their personal effects in goatskin or linen haversacks and were weighed down with a variety of camp kettles and other impedimenta. In the waggon train were a number of watch coats which were issued to the picquets and sentries at night but most of the men had to endure rain soaked clothing which faded and eventually rotted. Cavalry cut fascines every morning and they and the pioneers went ahead of the column dropping these in the very large pot holes and deeper ruts to prevent waggons and guns overturning.

To deceive enemy vedettes, Marlborough used an unorthodox march routine. The men were roused at very early hours, perhaps one or two o'clock in the morning, and were marched at speed for as long as they could sustain the pace. They then rested during the remainder of the day. Sometimes they kept this up for several days, then interrupted the onerous routine for one day to rest. By adopting this stop-go system Marlborough hoped to confuse any enemy scouts and to avoid the great clouds of dust which normally advertised the presence of armies on the move. Meantime General Overkirk reported signs that de Villeroi was to attack the meagre force which had been left in the Netherlands and sent an urgent despatch to Marlborough for either reinforcements or the return of his Army. Other messages reached Marlborough that Louis, the Grand Duke of Baden, who was commanding Imperial troops in the entrenched defences at Stollhofen, expected the French to attack him. He reached Coblenz on the 18th May, crossed the Rhine and then turned south to move through Neudorf Nastatten and Schwalbach. To placate the Dutch and Baden and to further confuse the French, Marlborough sent a pontoon team to the Rhine and they threw a bridge over the river near Phillipsburg. This had the desired effect. Both Allies and French thought his intention was to swing round to the west and cut back into the Palatinate and the Moselle Valley.

Marlborough continued to be much concerned with the health of his men. The gruelling march was taking its toll, and tired and dispirited infantrymen were dropping out and sinking in exhaustion by the roadside.

The Duke realised that, unless he could arrive at his destination with an army that was able, and indeed willing, to fight, the whole expedition would prove abortive. He therefore entrusted Cadogan with the task of organising small teams of Commissaries who galloped ahead of the marching men with only a light escort. Their task was to buy provisions and, more important, to set up camps at selected intervals along the route, find billets and see that the men had supplies of beer and wine. When the weary, mud or dust covered column trudged into the camping grounds all the men had to do was to boil their kettles and to set up their bivouacs. Marlborough was also much concerned with the condition of the mens' feet. Every camp site had its line of soldiers with stockings off holding up the soles of their feet for their officers inspection. It is said that the Duke would take invalids with blistered feet into his coach instead of leaving

them to the mercy of the local peasants. So unusual was this solicitude for his men that the common soldiers christened him "Corporal John".

As the army continued to move south the French, and the horrified Dutch, now guessed Marlborough's real intentions. He crossed the River Main near Kastel and reached the River Neckar by the 3rd June.

The French knew that they could not catch him in time. Their only hope lay in diverting French forces under de Tallard from the Rhine area, but by the time despatches reached the French Marshal, Marlborough had moved much further south. He had also been reinforced by troops from many of the German states including Hanover, Hesse, Mainz, Würzburg, together with the splendidly disciplined Prussian infantry and excellent mercenaries from Denmark.

At Heidelberg Marlborough scoured the city to buy new shoes for those men who had marched from the Netherlands and then, without pause, struck south again for Württemburg.

At Mundelscheim he met the legendary Prince Eugene of Savoy for the first time and the men struck up an instant friendship. The next day they rode to Gross Hepparch where, with much ceremony, the Prince inspected the British Regiments of Horse and the Dragoons. He said later that he was amazed to find the troops and their horses in such excellent condition.

Meantime de Tallard had not been idle; he managed to evade Louis of Baden and got some young reinforcement infantry through to Marsin. He then hurried north to meet Marshall de Villeroi in the Alsace region.

A meeting was arranged at which the three Coalition Commanders, Marlborough, Eugene and Baden, discussed future tactics in the light of the latest French moves. As a result, Eugene agreed to return to Stoffhofen to man the Grand Duke's trenched defences and to attempt to slow down any French advance. Baden was to stay with Marlborough and to share command with him on alternate days. This was an unsatisfactory arrangement from Marlborough's point of view but one he had to accept because Baden was determined to maintain protocol and resented being displaced as supreme Allied commander in the area.

The weather had broken again and the monsoon-like rains, which drenched the unhappy men, made the roads almost impassable. Even so, Marlborough constantly harangued the squadron and regimental commanders to hurry their men along and rode ahead of the main column with his cavalry. Soaked to the skin once again and with the horses and uniforms splattered with mud, the cavalry pushed on through Ebersbach and Göppingen to the heavily wooded Geislingen Pass, which they cleared by the 11th June. The infantry under the command of General of Foot, Charles Churchill, and the artillery train under Colonel Blood struggled to keep good time but the cumulative effects of the weather slowed their pace and the cavalry had to wait for them before they could be reunited near Gingen.

Having reformed, the great column snaked down into the valley of the Danube where, near Ulm, Marlborough and Baden had the pleasure of joining the Duke of Württemberg with the remaining element of their army which consisted of the Danish cavalry and some additional German infantry.

By the 22nd June Marlborough had reached Elchingen, having taken just under five weeks to march 300 miles from the Netherlands.

His intention was to cross the Danube into Bavaria and beat the Grand Elector in the field or, if possible, persuade him to leave the war. The army did not get much time to rest but swung north east, marching through Langenau, Balmershoffen and Amerdingen towards the important Danube river-crossing near the city of Dönauworth.

Because the weather slowed the march towards the river, the Elector of Bavaria and Marshal de Marsin managed to order their forces and move towards the city of Dillingen where there was a suitable fortified camp, but in doing so they reinforced Dönauworth with 10,000 infantry and 2,500 cavalry under the command of an experienced Piedmontese General, the Comte D'Arco.

The Count hastened to his new command where he began to throw up additional trench systems to bolster the meagre defence system which the town possessed. Time was not on his side, and these extra defences were never properly completed, especially those on the west side of the north face of the old hill fortress, (known as the "Schellenberg"), which was nearest to the town. Marlborough received intelligence of the improved defences to the town and knew that he had to destroy D'Arco's garrison if he hoped to gain a good bridgehead over the Danube and a base which might serve as a magazine for future operations in Bavaria.

2 Dönauworth and the Schellenberg

At three o'clock in the morning of the 2nd July Marlborough marched from his camp at Ebergmergen with the largely British left wing of the army, leaving the Grand Duke to follow him. By nine o'clock the two leading infantry brigades, which included British, Dutch and German battalions backed up by 35 squadrons of cavalry, were in sight of the Franco-Bavarian defences. Marlborough detached a "forlorn hope" of the grenadier company of the 1st British Foot Guards to move forward and try to break the entrenched defences. Meantime the cavalry had been ordered to dismount and to cut fascines. Each trooper carried one across his saddle. The intention was that the fascines should be passed to the infantry battalions as they went by and for the foot soldiers to drop them into the trenches so that the cavalry might pass over them without trouble.

An orderly from Eugene presently arrived to inform Marlborough that de Tallard was moving rapidly south through the Black Forest. Marlborough realised that he would have to take Dönauworth quickly to get his large force over the great river before the French arrived.

After by-passing the little village of Berg the British commenced the attack. The artillery was hauled and pushed into position. Blood opened fire on the hill and the 16 battalions began to move into the attack. The British Regiments included the 1st Foot Guards; Lt. General Ingoldsby's Regiment; Brig. General Meredith's Regiment; and the two battalions of the Royal Regiment. They advanced in four lines, each battalion three ranks deep, each man collecting his fascine as he passed the patient cavalry. Behind the cavalry, further battalions were moved up followed by the reserve.

The "forlorn hope" of sixty stalwart grenadiers of the 1st Foot Guards lead the way up to the trenches headed by Lord Mordaunt and under the command of Colonel Maunden. They were immediately subjected to intense fire from the defenders' artillery. Many men fell but although Lord Mordaunt and Colonel Maunden remained steadfastly in their front exhorting them to greater efforts and, waving them on with both hat and sword, these two officers remained unhurt.

The following lines of British, Dutch and Germans also came under heavy fire and became so excited by the fury of the defences that they prematurely threw their fascines into a depression in the ground which they had mistaken for the trenches.

Now the remnants of the "forlorn hope" and the leading ranks of the infantry battalions reached the parapets of the trenches and began struggling hand-to-hand with the French and Bavarians who manned them. The white and blue coated defenders fought so desperately that the impetus of the attack petered out and the men in the trenches, sensing the advantage sprang out of their defences and counter-attacked with bayonets, pushing their adversaries back down the slopes.

Fighting became very fierce on the slopes of the "Schellenberg", with both sides using bayonet and hanger to good effect. Bodies fell into the trenches and in their fury both sides trampled them into the mud, oblivious of the screams of the wounded. As more attacking reinforcements arrived D'Arco began to draw on the reserves allocated to the task of defending the side of the hill nearest to the town in an effort to bolster up his defences against the savage frontal attacks.

The brave defenders fought well, stemming the advances of the British and Dutch so effectively that Marlborough began to fear that he might not be able to secure his river crossing before nightfall. So tough did the defence become that he was forced to dismount some dragoons to support his infantry attacks. The Greys dismounted and hurried up the slopes to support their comrades, their fusils at the ready. Even as they came into action Baden came up and, without pause, flung in his 58 squadrons and 43 battalions of Imperial cavalry and infantry on D'Arco's exposed left flank. At first, D'Arco thought the new troops appearing near the town were French battalions coming to his aid. There is a contemporary account which mentions "white coated infantry" appearing on the left.

Baden poured his infantry and cavalry through the gap and then wheeled them around to attack the central entrenched positions in flank. For a time the defenders in the trenches managed to deploy to stem the attacks on their front and on

the flank but a magazine exploded somewhere near the town and this seemed to switch off their morale.

The dragoons were remounted and joined their comrades in the Regiments of Horse who now thundered in, through the intervals between the battalions, and fell on the hapless French and Bavarians who were struggling to retreat from the trenches. No mercy was shown to the totally disorganised defence. The cavalry hacked and clubbed at the retreating men and drove them towards the river where they jumped or were flung to their deaths.

Hundreds tried to escape across a flimsy pontoon bridge which D'Arco had flung up as a safeguard, in case retreat by the main bridge was denied him, but it broke under the weight of men and horses and pitched the miserable refugees into the brown swirling waters of the river, where they drowned.

Of the men who so gallantly fought in the "Schellenberg" trenches 5,000 were killed out of a force of 12,000 but Marlborough's losses were also very heavy; approximately 1,350 killed with a further 3,700 wounded. The British regiments suffered particularly badly and lost 88 officers and 1,200 men. Officer casualties were proportionately high and four General Officers were killed with a further twelve wounded. Of Baden's force, the Grand Duke's own Regiment of Baden suffered the most losses.

Marlborough and Baden later rode through the shattered defences to inspect the silent town and viewed the prisoners, cannon, baggage and stores which had been taken. That night the heavy rain returned and Marlborough's sodden and tired army moved back to bivouac at Ebermergen.

This action had enabled Marlborough to cross the Danube and enter Bavaria. It placed him between the French and Bavarians and Vienna and his first objective had been obtained. The Elector of Bavaria subsequently retired to Augsburg on the west bank of the River Lech, where he knew the defences were good and where the river would help protect his army from a sudden attack by Marlborough. For a while Marlborough pursued him but soon accepted that to set seige to Augsburg would be playing into his enemy's hands. For if the Elector could delay Marlborough until de Tallard could force march through into Bavaria a tremendous advantage would be gained. The Elector had detached part of his Electoral Army to Munich to guard his estates and consequently weakened his force but had no intention of leaving Augsburg.

Marlborough did not wait; instead he started a campaign of arson and pillage in the Bavarian countryside. Villages, farms and crops were set ablaze, but to no avail, as the Elector remained firmly behind the River Lech. Marlborough wrote later that he hated carrying out this atrocity but felt at the time that there was no other course left open to him. There seems little doubt that the Grand Duke of Baden found the whole action very distasteful indeed and the two commanders probably quarreled over the issue.

Marlborough received further intelligence that Eugene was experiencing trouble on the north bank of the Danube. De Tallard was causing him to retreat along the bank of the river, unable to resist the vastly superior French forces brought against him. The intention of the French commander was clear: to try and reach the Elector at or near Augsburg and to cut off Marlborough's retreat and lines of communication.

Marlborough was consequently forced to break off his ravage of the Bavarian countryside in order to succour Eugene. He immediately despatched thirty squadrons of cavalry to reinforce the Prince and then left the Augsburg area with the rest of the army to strike north towards Ingolstadt to secure an additional bridgehead for a return over the Danube in case he was forced to retreat that way.

By August 1st, de Marsin and the Elector, aware that de Tallard was close at hand, united their forces and began to move north with 56,000 men towards Eberbach. At about the same time, Eugene had reached Schrobenhausen by a series of forced marches and managed to gallop to meet Marlborough to discuss future plans while his 18,000 Imperial and Prussian infantry rested. Marlborough and Eugene knew that time was growing short. Beside the large force that de Tallard, de Marsin and the Elector could now bring against them, they heard that Marshal de Villeroi had begun to move south through the Palatinate with another large French army of 46,000 men. They managed to convince the conservative Baden that he would be performing an excellent duty to the cause by besieging Ingolstadt to secure their bridgehead and allocated 24 battalions, thirty-one squadrons and thirty of the guns for the task. By the 7th August the French and Bavarians had united, and de Tallard, de Marsin and the Elector had re-crossed the Danube and reached Lauingen. The great army then moved onto the plain east of Dillingen between the villages of Blenheim and Oberglau near Höchstädt. At this stage, de Tallard, de Marsin and the Elector were in joint command of the combined armies and this affected the argument which erupted between the French and Bavarian commanders over the quality of their position. De Marsin and the Elector could see no fault with it but de Tallard was not happy. He tried to convince his colleagues that they should seek a more advantageous field but after consulting some of the other staff of the French and Bavarian commands they decided to stay where they were.

Meantime, Marlborough moved his force back towards Dönauworth and then split them into wings once more to facilitate the crossing of the river. Part crossed at Merxheim and the others struck through Rain, crossed the Lech and then over the Danube by Dönauworth. By the 11th August the whole Coalition Army was over the river and had linked up with Eugene's Imperial and Prussian infantry.

Apparently completely oblivious of the proximity of their enemies, the French and Bavarians rested in their tents across the four miles of open land between Lutzingen and Blenheim. Their army consisted of 143 squadrons and 70 battalions, a force of 56,000 men with 90 guns.

Eugene and Marlborough rode to the village of Tapfheim and climbed the church spire. Armed with spy glasses they eagerly sought out the French camp and the order of encampment.

On their return to their tents they wrote orders for their staff and sent Aides with messages to the various brigade, battalion and squadron commanders informing them that the army would march in the small hours of the next day. The men cleaned their arms, prepared bridles and saddlery for action and laid down to snatch a few hours sleep. Some British battalions were moved out and marched to Schwenningen where they were posted to guard the pass into the plain before the river Nebel and protect the advance of the allied march the next morning.

About one o'clock on the cold morning of the 13th August 1704, the two commanders took leave of each other and repaired to their separate wings of the army. The drums beat "assembly" and the polygot army of British, Dutch, German, Imperial and Danish regiments folded their tents, put out their fires and began to manoeuvre into nine great marching columns. On the left, the British with some German battalions; in the centre more British but principally the Dutch; and on the right, the Imperial troops with the efficient Danes and Prussian infantry.

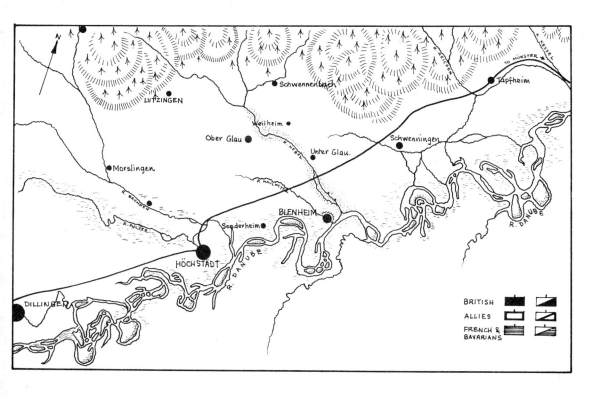

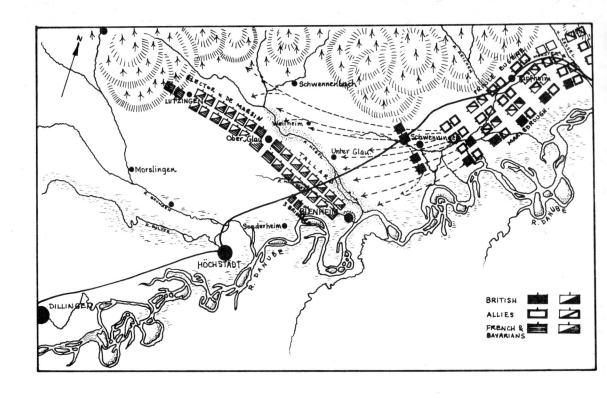

3 The Battle

Marlborough had 178 squadrons of cavalry and 65 battalions of infantry totalling 52,000 men supported by 66 guns. The right of the army was commanded by his brother, Charles Churchill, Marlborough commanded the centre and Prince Eugene the right wing. From Münster the nine columns advanced, past Tapfheim, crossing the Reichen brook, marching past the north side of slumbering Schwenningen where they picked up the remaining British battalions and then began to spray out, the left towards Gremheim and Blenheim; the centre towards the little hamlet of Unter Glau and the right towards Schwennenbach and Weilheim. They crossed the Kessel stream by means of a hastily constructed pontoon bridge and proceeded west to the River Nebel, a shallow marsh banked river which flowed into the Danube.

The French and Bavarian army slept on, their Generals apparently unaware still of the danger which faced them.

By six o'clock the attacking columns had deployed into line in their allotted positions on the field. When forward picquets made contact with the French the alarmed sentries sent word to their officers that "Malbrook" was upon them.

The French officers, roused by their servants, hastily flung on their clothes and emerged from their tents. On the further side of the river the thick white mist of early morning was being drawn up into a clear blue sky and on the sunlit plain to their front they saw with amazement the army of Marlborough and Eugene, wheeling and marching into position. Their enemy was close enough for the bewildered French to see the colours of the uniforms, and see the devices on the fluttering standards and guidons.

When de Tallard was informed that the Coalition army was so close he was, at first, unperturbed. He still expected Marlborough and Eugene to carry out the classic manoeuvres of avoiding direct confrontation and attempting to proceed north west to Nördlingen 'en route' back to the Rhine.

To the north west, the open stubble covered land on which the French were encamped was protected by pine wooded hills behind the village of Lutzingen. To the south east, the village of Blenheim reached almost to the steep bank of the River Danube and midway between these two defence points, was the village of Oberglau. To their front, and between them and

Marlborough and Eugene, the ground sloped down gently to water meadows and marshes which bordered the shallow River Nebel. Near the Danube two mills bordered the river on the eastern side.

Watching the great army of the British and her allies swinging across his front and beginning to form up into battle formations, de Tallard finally realised that they intended to fight and that he had no time to find other ground. He lost no time in setting his own army in motion, breaking camp, and spreading out across the wide plain between Lutzingen and the Danube. Blenheim itself was a large cluttered village containing many fine gabled houses with painted stucco walls in the Bavarian style, and with mills, farms and yards enclosed with high walls. De Tallard placed nine battalions of his best French infantry regiments in the village supported by 12 squadrons of dismounted dragoons whose horses had died with disease. His troops were ordered to make defences around the villages with palisades and overturned waggons. On the slightly higher ground to the south west of the village, de Tallard posted three further brigades totalling 18 French battalions. His instructions to General de Clerambault, the village commander, were explicit: on no account were these troops to be brought up, or moved into the village, without his instructions.

To the north west of Blenheim and between the village and Oberglau, de Tallard placed a mass of cavalry including several regiments of the élite Gens d'armes. This force of 64 squadrons, containing some of the finest of the French regiments of horse, dressed in splendid uniforms and mounted on huge black horses, was spread out in two extended lines and put under the command of an experienced Swiss cavalry officer named Lt. General Beat-Jacques, Count of Zurlauben. In support of this elongated force of cavalry de Tallard placed only nine infantry battalions, mainly composed of very young and inexperienced conscript soldiers, some of whom he had pushed through from the Alsace to reinforce de Marsin.

Oberglau was a small village at a similar distance from the river as Blenheim. The commander of that post was the French General, Jules Marquis de Blainville, whose force comprised fourteen battalions of infantry, some posted in the village and the others deployed in and around the outskirts.

De Marsin and the Elector of Bavaria commanded the left wing which comprised 67 squadrons of French and Bavarian cavalry and twelve battalions of mixed infantry. The French and Bavarians had little time now to allow a leisurely consideration of the deployment of their army. Having, literally, to step from their beds and hurry their battalion and squadron commanders into position, de Tallard, de Marsin and the Elector had made a grave error in not allocating sufficient infantry in their centre. Their order of battle had been drawn up in what Trevelyan calls "the order of encampment" with all the cavalry spread across two miles of the centre of the field.

Presumably de Tallard considered that by standing his line back from the low lying and treacherous swamp land by the River Nebel he could fight on firmer ground and would be better able to manoeuvre his cavalry to destroy badly formed infantry and cavalry emerging with difficulty from the water meadows. However, de Tallard had stretched the centre of the French-Bavarian forces into a very tenuous link across the battlefield and their order of battle had produced two separate armies rather than one homogeneous force under a cohesive command.

Because the land to the north west of his marching columns was difficult to move through, Marlborough had to wait for Prince Eugene to reach his position before their plan could be set in action. Meantime he ordered his men to lie down to avoid the enemy artillery. Passing by and through the hamlets of Vulperstat and Swenbach, Eugene marched his Austrians, Danes and Prussians as fast as the construction of a pontoon bridge over a loop in the Nebel would allow.

16

cont. p. 33

British General

British Officer of Foot Guards

British Sergeant of Foot Guards

British Dragoon

British Artilleryman

British Infantryman

Danish Infantryman

Dutch Infantryman

Dutch Officer

25

Austrian Infantryman

Prussian Officer

French General

French Gen d'Arme

French Infantryman

French Infantry Officer

Bavarian Cuirrassier

While waiting for Eugene, Marlborough organised drumhead services for the various contingents at the head of the battalions and detachments made rough pontoon bridges over the Nebel. By 12 o'clock the French artillery was heavily in action and ball and "partridge" (grape) shot was causing Marlborough much concern.

By 12.30 Prince Eugene sent an Aide to inform his colleague that he was ready. The two armies were now drawn up in full view of each other. From de Tallard's position could be seen the great blocks of red, blue, grey, yellow and white, interspersed with the bright colours of the drummers and trumpeters. Through his spyglass Marlborough could see the masses of white clad French infantry, in and behind Blenheim, urgently putting the finishing touches to their barricades and palisades.

In the centre, he could see the extended lines of the French cavalry, resplendent in scarlet and blue, and mounted on magnificent black horses. As he moved his glass to his right he could see the great blocks of blue and buff which were the Bavarians and beyond them, the blue haze of the pine covered hills beyond Lutzingen.

According to the rigid and formalised tactics of the time, the troops were dressed into line by the hoarse shouts of their officers and sergeants and to the 'flam' and ruffle of the drums. The cavalry kettledrums and trumpets also sounded while Ensigns and Cornets flourished their standards and guidons to indicate the position of the rallying points for their men.

By now the French had fired the two mills and farm buildings which bordered the river and the black smoke from these and from the blazing straw and hay ricks was adding to the acrid powder smoke which was drifting over the opposing armies. In front of Blenheim, dismounted French dragoons were still hammering in the last touches to the palisades which faced the river and many of the buildings in the village had been fired. Marlborough ordered the first move and his brother, Charles Churchill, ordered the intrepid Lord "Salamander" Cutts

to lead out his infantry, supported by Hanoverian and Hessian battalions, towards the Blenheim defences. They stepped off to the beat of the drum, marching slowly down through the shallow water meadows into the river, forded it, and began to help each other from the morass on the other side. In the centre Marlborough began to move the Dutch infantry and his cavalry down towards the river.

By one o'clock, the British battalions, now in a unique four line formation, were almost clear of the low lying swamp and had dressed their ranks. Once more the drums beat and they began to recommence their slow march up the gently rising ground towards the Blenheim palisades. Their men were falling in swathes from the heavy French artillery fire and musket fire from behind the barricades. They passed the blazing mills and marched steadily towards the village, line following line. Brigadier Lord Rowe galloped up to the front of the marching lines and shouted to his men to hold their fire until they reached the defences. Still marching with shouldered arms the British infantry moved on, suffering very heavy casualties. When the attackers were about thirty paces from the barricades, the French infantry fired a volley and great gaps appeared in the British front ranks. Brigadier Rowe had now reached the defences and thrust his sword through the palisade calling on his men to open fire. The British fired a volley and rushed the palisades, shooting and stabbing through the wooden stakes but the French, comparatively safe behind their defences, replied with such heavy fire that the British were compelled to fall back. As they did so, Lord Rowe fell mortally wounded and two other senior officers, who ran to his aid, fell dead across his body.

As the British retreated they were attacked by emerging French infantry and, more significantly, by squadrons of the scarlet uniformed Gens d'armes, who swept around the perimeter of the village and took them in flank.

During this savage attack the Gens d'armes managed to capture the colours of Brigadier

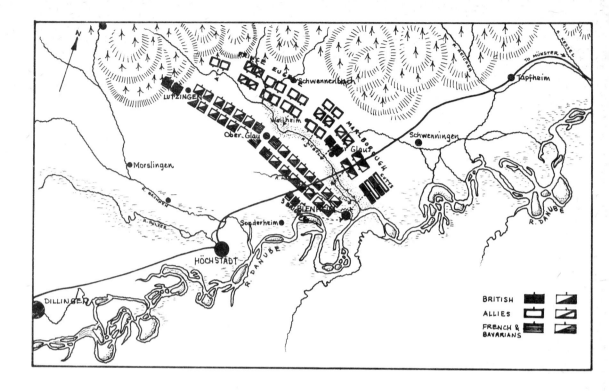

Rowe's Regiment but were attacked almost immediately by the Hessian battalions who coolly fired into the slow moving mass of horses and forced them to relinquish their prizes, which were immediately returned to the British Regiment.

Further squadrons of Gens d'armes were now moving in to engage Lord Cutts and to counter the threat, General Churchill called for help from General Charles Lumley with the British cavalry.

Lumley was engaged in supervising the clearance of the treacherous swampy ground and reforming his squadrons. Seeing Cutt's acute problem, he called on Colonel Francis Palmes to take out five squadrons to his aid. The French cavalry were arrogantly engaged in performing their almost casual drill, moving up, firing their pistols, then wheeling aside to enable the next line to perform the same operation, when the five British squadrons smashed into their eight, charging home with the sword. As a result, the French squadrons, most of whom were young nobles and considered to be the flower of their cavalry, were flung into confusion and to de Tallard's dismay, were forced to beat a hasty retreat suffering severe casualties.

Lord Cutts now ordered his second brigade, which included the Royal Regiment, Churchill's Regiment, Webb's Regiment, Howe's Regiment, the Earl of Derby's Regiment, Meredith's Regiment and Ferguson's Regiment, to attack the village in a similar manner. Led out by Ferguson himself, their attack was a repeat of the onslaught by Rowe's Brigade and ended in much the same way, except that some of the British and the reserves of Dutch infantry managed to establish themselves in the outskirts. In the village, where many burning buildings were causing unbearable conditions for the tightly massed French battalions, the commander Lt. General Phillipe Marquis de Clerambault appeared to have lost his nerve. Fearing a third frontal attack and considering that, if it came, his men would give way he called in those eighteen reserve battalions of infantry which his commander had specifically instructed should be left where they were. When these additional men had marched in, a proper deployment of his battalions became practically impossible. The village was crammed with nearly 12,000 inactive men from some of the best infantry regiments in the French Army. Seeing the terrible casualties suffered by Lord Cutts' brigades in attacking the village, Marlborough sent an Aide to tell him to keep his men up as close to the village as possible but to order them to lie down and wait, taking advantage of every hollow in the ground. His first objective had been achieved for, although the British and Dutch had not taken Blenheim, their sustained attacks had resulted in the infantry reserve being drawn in and away from the vital position in the field and the garrison was contained.

On the right, Prince Eugene was having a difficult time containing de Marsin and the Elector. Their forces greatly outnumbered his own and, although the Prussian infantry and the young Dutch battalions were fighting magnificently, the Imperial troops were being severely mauled by the excellent regiments of Bavarian cuirassiers. His troops were suffering heavy casualties but the effect of his unselfish action was to contain the entire French left wing, depriving them of the opportunity to detach reinforcements to Blenheim or the centre.

Since Blenheim no longer offered a threat, Marlborough ordered the Hanoverian battalions to be moved over from the left to join the Prince of Holstein-Beck who was ordered to attack Oberglau with his infantry brigade.

Eleven battalions were dressed and began to move slowly forward to the village. However, the commander of Oberglau, de Blainville, was a different opponent to de Clerambault. Instead of waiting for the attack to reach him he sallied out from behind his defences with his forward battalions (including the Irish emigré regiments in the French service who were known as the "Wild Geese"). Their volleys and bayonet charges caused the Prince's attack to falter. As they began to move back towards the bad ground they were attacked by more French cavalry in flank and, for a while, the position in the centre appeared to have swung to de Tallard's advantage. However the French cavalry's initial success was again badly exploited and Marlborough had time to bring over the Hanoverians, Dutch reserve and further artillery thereby reversing the advantage. The gallant French and their Irish battalions were forced back into the village.

While this confused fighting was taking place in front of Oberglau, Marlborough was despatching orders via his Aides to bring over the remainder of his forces. He had seven further infantry battalions to deploy in the centre and his fresh cavalry were clearing the bad ground.

At about 2.15 a further French cavalry attack strongly pressed the right flank of his centre and they penetrated far enough to unsettle the balance once more in that sector of the field. Indeed, the situation became grave enough for Marlborough to send a dragoon to Prince Eugene with an urgent appeal for assistance. The calm Prince had much confidence in his "twin" general and although still hard pressed he sent him a brigade of Austrian cuirassiers. These fresh cavalry, anxious to atone for the poor results of their fellow countrymen in dealing with the Bavarian heavy cavalry, arrived at the gallop and smashed home their furious attack into the flank of the French cavalry with such great enthusiasm that they flung them into utter confusion. At this time, Eugene was still having difficulty in holding sustained attacks of the Bavarians on the right flank but the seven battalions of Danish infantry and eleven battalions of Prussians were performing magnificently under great pressure.

Since bringing the remainder of his reserve over the river, Marlborough was able to take advantage of a temporary respite in the action in the centre and around Blenheim. After a while, even the heavy attacks by the Bavarians and the counter-attacks by Eugene seemed to have almost petered out.

By about 4 o'clock Marlborough had finally managed to deploy his entire centre on the French side of the River Nebel wedging it between the inactive French battalions in Blenheim and de Marsin on the right. He therefore ordered General Lumley to trot the still fresh British cavalry over from his left to the centre to join the patient squadrons already formed for attack. Marlborough then had a superb force of 81 squadrons of cavalry, supported by 18 battalions of infantry, poised in the centre. The cavalry were almost entirely unused, dressed up into attacking formations with their kettledrummers and trumpeters formed up in their rear ready to sound the order to advance. Opposing this large force, de Tallard could only produce the remnants of the 64 squadrons of his centre most of whom had already seen much action and were viewing with some trepidation the great mass of horsemen to their front. A French staff officer galloped furiously into Blenheim with orders that de Clerambault must release two brigades of his infantry instantly, for service in the centre. The hysterical commander refused to release them and drove the French staff from the village with abuse, curses and threats. When they returned empty handed de Tallard realised that without adequate reinforcements he would face Marlborough not only with inferior cavalry but also a brigade of young and inexperienced infantry. His answer was a last desperate charge by the Gens d'armes and, before the Allied cavalry could be properly set in motion, they had to contest this frenzied assault by the tired squadrons of the élite enemy horse. For a time it seemed that the advance of Marlborough's cavalry was to be checked but the infantry battalions formed in their rear were rapidly brought up and began to attack the French flanks and Major General Orkney placed himself at the head of the cavalry and rallied them.

The young French infantry in the centre had meantime formed a marching square to repulse the expected cavalry attack and now became horribly exposed to Colonel Blood's centre battery of nine guns which poured "partridge" and case shot into their tattered ranks. Orkney's men moved up and also began to fire by platoons into the ranks of the young Frenchmen. For a time it seemed that courage might be enough and that the French square could hold; then to eye witnesses it seemed that it disappeared, almost entirely swept away by the tremendous fire from artillery and muskets.

Now was the moment for the Dutch and British cavalry and they swept through, starting their charge at the trot, knee to knee and gradually gaining momentum up the gentle slope until they crashed into the waiting French cavalry at a furious gallop, smashing their front ranks and forcing them back into a confused mass until, engulfed and encircled by slashing steel, they attempted to break for the west and gallop to safety. But, so tightly pressed were the French that, in some cases they were unable to lift their sword arms, to defend themselves. The frenzied mass of horses and men were driven back, suffering heavily from the hacking and stabbing swords of their adversaries until, totally disorganised, they reached the steep banks of the Danube near Sonderheim where some 3,000 slid down the 20ft. banks and were drowned trying to escape by swimming the river.

Meanwhile, de Tallard had seen that his only chance lay with the still passive infantry brigades locked in blazing Blenheim village and tried to gallop with his staff to bring them out.

Misfortune again struck de Tallard when his entourage was neatly intercepted by a squadron of Hessian Dragoons and he and his staff were captured. On the left wing of the French position de Marsin and the Elector had been watching the fluctuating battle in the centre of the field through their glasses and judged that the outcome could no longer be in doubt. Trevelyan puts it that ". . . the remoter distances of the plain soon appeared to be sprinkled with

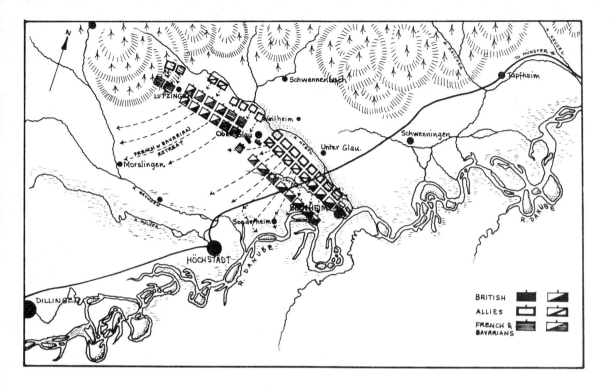

innumerable moving spots, all making like insects in desperate haste towards the brushwood line of the Danube or the tall sentinel Schloss of Höchstädt".

Marlborough's efforts to curtail his cavalry's enthusiastic pursuit of the French were to no avail and he judged that he would have little time before dusk to muster a sufficiently large force to successfully pursue de Marsin and the Elector. He therefore concentrated his next actions on Oberglau and Blenheim.

Oberglau was in fact no longer a threat and resistance in that area had virtually disintegrated, although some squadrons of his cavalry were mopping up the remnants of the bewildered French and Irish regiments around the village and herding them off the field.

Lord Orkney, having seen the collapse of the French centre, had wheeled his British regiments to join Cutts' and General Churchill's troops on the left flank around Blenheim.

Churchill ordered Orkney to take his and Ingoldsby's Regiments and march them around the perimeter of the village, over the Maulweyer stream, to the banks of the Danube. Churchill's Regiment straddled the stream and he ordered the troops to face inwards. The British now had a ring of steel round the village. The French commander, de Clerambault, whose actions had been quite irrational for much of the battle, now completely broke down and leaped onto his horse. He furiously galloped from the village, through the astonished British lines and urged his horse into the river where he drowned. The British were now anxious to get possession of the village before nightfall. They realised that the large force of unused French infantry within the village still had the power to march out and

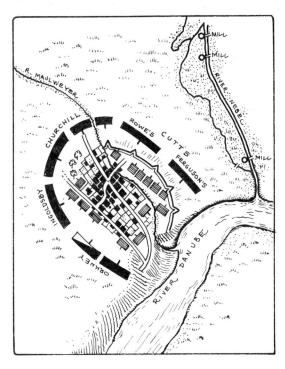

SKETCH MAP OF THE VILLAGE OF BLENHEIM
AT THE END OF THE BATTLE.

Ordering his drummer to "beat a parley" he boldly walked out in front of his troops and demanded to speak to the French officer in charge. The young French officer who came forward to speak with him was a Brigadier General named de Nonville. After some discussion with the wily Scots Lord he agreed to order his men to lay down their arms and, at the same time, Ingoldsby was achieving the same result with the other French Brigadier General. The surrender was not accepted with good grace by the rank and file and many of the other French officers became excited. At one time the whole delicate negotiation seemed in doubt and when a British Aide pulled the colours from the hands of an excited young ensign he received a sword thrust for his pains. The French Commander in the village at this time was the Marquis de Blansac and his immediate reaction to the surrender proposal was to refuse but, after further discussions with Lord Orkney and his Aide, he reluctantly agreed as no other course of action was left to him, and was finally escorted from the blazing village.

On the further side of Blenheim the weary soldiers of Rowe's and Ferguson's Brigades were reforming for another attack. When they heard of the surrender they sank back to the ground, all but spent.

Behind the barricades the young officers of the élite infantry Regiment of Navarre, enraged at the surrender, ceremonially burnt their standards rather than let them be captured. Twenty battalions of French infantry and twelve squadrons of dismounted French dragoons marched from the village and piled their arms and standards while the smoke-grimed British and Dutch regiments formed up and saluted.

By 9 o'clock all fighting had ceased. Marlborough had achieved a remarkable and complete victory and the Grand Army of Louis XIV, for decades considered the invincible force in Europe, had been soundly thrashed and outmanoeuvred by an inferior force and with great loss.

For the loss of nearly 13,000 officers and men,

possibly escape. On the Nebel side of the village Lord Cutts' men again advanced on the palisades. They were repulsed once more but each time they came forward more men managed to infiltrate the outskirts. Ingoldsby's and Orkney's Regiments managed to reach the churchyard on the west side but could not gain entry because of the fierce resistance by the defenders crammed behind the high brick wall which surrounded it. The Greys, again dismounted, helped prevent the French leave the churchyard and escape into the narrow streets and Ingoldsby's men began to move in, using their street firing technique to push the French into the centre.

Orkney, seeing two French battalions in his front forming ready to attack, and realising that this could be disastrous for the weary British infantry, used subtler methods to overcome them.

the Duke and Prince Eugene had destroyed an Army of 60,000 inflicting 20,000 casualties and taking 14,000 prisoners, including the Commander-in-Chief and other Generals. In the process, the gallant British regiments, who had laboured all day to contain a greatly superior force of fine French infantry bottled up inside Blenheim, had lost 670 killed and had 1,500 wounded.

Three hundred standards and richly embroidered banners, kettledrums, and 60 cannon and mortars had been taken and the entire French baggage with camp stores captured. That night the vanquished French survivors were bivouaced on the plain and guarded by the weary British. Marlborough later met de Tallard and the other French senior officers to discuss their future and, as a result, de Tallard was sent to England where he lived happily for many years.

Marlborough, tired and smoke-grimed, eventually managed to sit in his tent and scribble a hasty note to his wife, using the only piece of paper available, an old tavern bill: —

"I have no time to say more but beg you will give my duty to the Queen and let her know her Army has had a glorious victory. Monsr. Tallard and two other generals are in my coach and I am following the rest. The bearer, my Aide de Camp Coll. Parke, will give her an account of what has passed. I shall do it in a day or two by another more at large".

The remnants of the Franco-Bavarian left wing under the Elector of Bavaria and Marshal de Marsin retreated from the battlefield in good order but their march rapidly developed into a rout. The German peasantry through whose country they passed, lost no time in attacking the column whenever the occasion presented itself. The French in turn exacted every kind of atrocity on the German countryside, pillaging and looting. By the time they reached Ulm it was said that there were only 250 of the officers left, in four regiments, who were neither wounded or killed and that four regiments of dragoons had only a handful of their original strength.

It was estimated that they lost nearly 40,000 by the end of August. Most of the Elector's Bavarian troops were disbanded or crept back to their villages where they swiftly removed all traces of their former military life.

The Elector himself, with a faithful handful of his Army, retreated with de Marsin, suffering all the ignominies of defeat (he eventually became Vice-General of the Netherlands).

Before the French reached Strasbourg they had been even further decimated by the marauding bands of Austrian hussars who constantly snapped at their heels. Marlborough first went to see the Emperor Leopold in Vienna where he was received in triumph and given the Princedom of Mundelscheim in gratitude for saving the Empire from disaster.

Marlborough then followed the French retreat, re-crossing the Rhine near Phillipsbourg and organising the Austrian siege of Landau in the Palatinate. Not waiting for the result of that action, he moved on back into the Moselle area where he set siege to, and took, Trêves.

By November his weary troops were ready to go into winter quarters and Fortescue records that the British infantry regiments had been much weakened by the campaign, not only by their strenuous marches but also by the battle of Blenheim. Of the former fourteen battalions of foot who had left the Netherlands in May so few men were left that they had to re-organise them into seven! The Duke, having satisfied himself that his men were to be well cared for during the winter to come, set sail for England where he was set ashore on the 14th December.

Marlborough proceeded in triumph from Greenwich to visit the Queen. Delighted to see her champion returned and with the splendid way in which he triumphed over the all-powerful Louis she showered him with gifts. The Royal Manor of Woodstock was given to him and the beautiful Blenheim Palace erected there at Anne's expense. He became the Colonel of Her Majesties Life Guards.

Appendix 1

Early 18th Century Battle Formations

The deployment of large armies into formations from which they were able to attack or repel attacks by similar forces took a great deal of time. It was common for hours to be spent bringing the armies onto the chosen field of battle and then wheeling the battalions and squadrons into line.

It was useful to march onto the field in columns, each rank marching five or six abreast. When the columns reached within about 200 ft. of the enemy they would wheel, the battalions marching along a parallel front with the enemy, until they reached their allotted positions. When they reached their posts the battalions or squadrons halted, faced the enemy and their ranks were dressed by the Troop or Company officers and sergeants.

Only when the great masses of men and horse had finished manoeuvring, and their respective commanding officers had reported to the Aides that all was ready, did the General Officers ride onto the field and take up their respective positions.

Movement was slow, indeed the word "slow" is frequently found in the drill books of the period. The complicated evolutions had to be carried out at a steady pace. This had two advantages, first the men had time to remember the very complicated drills and secondly it avoided breaks in the smooth continuity of the movements, which could easily cause confusion in the transformation of column into line or line into square. Any break in the unity of the massed formation could present sharp eyed enemy commanders with the opportunity to catch them in confusion, with fatal results.

Troops were therefore drilled remorselessly until they achieved near perfection. Harsh punishments were meted out to any man who was caught moving incorrectly, putting his unit and comrades at risk. An infantry battalion in standing or manoeuvring square or in line, calm and executing their drill with machine-like precision, could be formidable. On the other hand an ill-disciplined unit responding sluggishly to drum or order and with little respect for its drill sergeants could be a menace, not only to itself, but to the entire army.

It was not until the American War of Independence when the British infantry and their German mercenaries had to face skilled individual riflemen using natural cover and self-discipline, that the old drill book techniques began to be questioned. However, during the period under review, these systems were still being developed and would not reach full maturity until the genius of Frederick the Great of Prussia brough this type of warfare to it's peak.

The British system of battle formation involved the use of a front line of infantry battalions spaced out with either single guns or batteries of guns placed between them. Behind the front line of infantry, squadrons of cavalry were placed in reserve which, in turn, were backed by a second line of spaced infantry battalions. At the rear was posted a reserve of cavalry.

The Imperial (Austrian) Army used a line comprising alternate infantry battalions and cavalry squadrons backed by a similar line and with a third in reserve. They often utilised "chevau de frise" defences and an old drill book of the period shows a fiercely moustached sergeant instructing a line of white coated infantry to thrust pikes through a long baulk of timber to provide these defences. In the background of the plate a battalion can be seen exercising this method with a line of skirmishers in front,

The French favoured a system in which the infantry battalions were strung out in one long line six men deep with their batteries of guns placed at regular intervals along the front. Their cavalry would be massed in deep columns by troops on the flanks. The second line was a repeat of the first.

Appendix 2

The British Contingent at Blenheim

THE REGIMENTS

Lt. General Lumley's Regiment of Horse (3 squadrons)
Commander: Lt. Col. Thos. Crowther

Major General Wood's Regiment of Horse (2 squadrons)
Commander: Lt. Col. J. Featherstonehaugh

Brigadier General Cadogan's Regiment of Horse (1 squadron)
Commander: Major R. Napier

Lieut. General Wyndham's Regiment of Horse (2 squadrons)
Commander: Lt. Col. F. Palmes

The Duke of Schomberg's Regiment of Horse (2 squadrons)
Commander: Lt. Col. Charles De Sybourg

Lord John Hay's Regiment of Dragoons (1 squadron)
Commander: Lt. Col. George Preston

Major General Ross's Regiment of Dragoons (3 squadrons)
Commander: Lt. Col. O. Wynne

THE HOUSEHOLD TROOPS

1st Regiment of Foot Guards
Commander: Lt. Col. H. Withers

THE REGIMENTS OF FOOT

The Royal Regiment of Foot — 1st Battalion
Commander: Colonel The Earl of Orkney Lt.

The Royal Regiment of Foot — 2nd Battalion
Commander: Major A. Hamilton

General Churchill's Regiment of Foot
Commander: Lt. Col. Peyton

Brigadier General Webb's Regiment of Foot
Commander: Lt. Col. R. Sutton

Lord North and Grey's Regiment of Foot
Commander: Lt. Col. H. Groves

Brigadier General Howe's Regiment of Foot
Commander: Lt. Col. W. Breton

The Earl of Derby's Regiment of Foot
Commander: Lt. Col. H. Hamilton

Brigadier General Hamilton's Regiment of Foot
Commander: Lt. Col. R. Sterne

Brigadier General Rowe's Regiment of Foot
Commander: Lt. Col. J. Dalyell

Lt. General Ingoldsby's Regiment of Foot (also called the Welsh Regt. of Fuzileers)
Commander: Lt. Col. J. Sabine

The Duke of Marlborough's Regiment of Foot
Commander: Lt. Col. W. Tatton

Brigadier General Ferguson's Regiment of Foot (also called the Cameronian Regt.)
Commander: Lt. Col. A. Livingston

Brigadier General Meredith's Regiment of Foot
Commander: Lt. Col. T. Bellow

THE HORSE

At full strength a Regiment of Horse was divided into nine troops of about 60 men each. On campaign these nine troops were grouped into three squadrons. However, many regiments were well under strength, and were grouped into two, or even one squadron.

Headquarters Establishment
1 Colonel, 1 Lt. Colonel, 1 Major, 1 Adjutant, 1 Chaplain, 1 Surgeon, 1 Kettledrummer.

The Troop was commanded by a Captain with a Lieutenant as his second in command. Each troop also had a Cornet and a Quartermaster. The rank and file of a troop consisted of three Corporals of Horse, two Trumpeters and 40-60 Troopers.

The British cavalry regiments formed up with a front of three troops (1 squadron) with a further three troops behind them, then an interval, and a further three troops.

The drill book quotes: —
"The interval or distance between each squadron is to be equal to the ground one squadron stands on".

Four important orders are given: —
"Open Order". "The distance between each rank when drawn up into a squadron; which distance must be equal to half the front of the squadron".
"Order". "The distance the ranks are to be at when the squadrons march; which is equal to one third of its front".
"Close Order". "The distance the ranks are to be at when moving up to the enemy; which distance is that four men may just wheel round in".
"Close to the group". "As close as they can be; in which position they are to charge".

The complete evolution of the regiments of horse and dragoons would fill a book but an impression of the complexity of the manoeuvres and movements involved can be gained from the number of movements needed to form up the squadrons ready to charge the enemy. Sixteen orders had to be shouted by the squadron commanders forming them to the centres, doubling the files, wheeling the files to the right or left, ordering the officers to take post at the head of their troops, drawing swords and finishing with the order: —
"Squadrons, have a care to march forward — March!"

The drill for handling carbines and fusils were equally complicated and involved some fifty, very lengthy evolutions, many of which consisted of three or more individual movements. The drill for the regiments of Horse and Dragoons differed little except that for the Dragoons there was also a complicated foot drill which reflected their quasi-infantry status. A further pointer is the fact that the Dragoon firearm is called the "firelock" rather than "carbine".

THE DRAGOONS

The Dragoon Regiments at this time were invariably considered to be mounted infantry and their establishment reflected this role.

Headquarters Establishment
1 Colonel, 1 Lt. Colonel, 1 Major, 1 Adjutant, 1 Chaplain, 1 Surgeon.
Each Troop consisted of two Sergeants, three Corporals, two Hautboys who doubled as Drummers, and 38-54 Troopers.

THE FOOT

The Strength of the British Infantry Regiments was as follows:
The 1st Foot Guards and all Regiments of Foot, except the Royal Regiment, had one battalion.
The Royal Regiment had two battalions during the 1704 campaign.
The British infantry battalions had twelve companies one of which was the grenadier company, an élite formation which had the right to form on the right of the line at reviews and parades. Some regiments had thirteen companies.

The Battalion Headquarters comprised:

1 Colonel, 1 Lt. Colonel, 1 Major, 1 Adjutant, 1 Chaplain, 1 Surgeon and 1 Surgeon's Mate.

Each of the companies was commanded by a Captain.

In most regiments the Lt. Colonel and the Major also carried the rank of Company Commander and drew pay for the rank.

Besides the Captain each company had a Lieutenant and an Ensign. In the grenadier companies there were two Lieutenants.

The strength of the rank and file of a company was two sergeants, two corporals and about 50 privates.

However, a scrutiny of the Blenheim Roll shows that many regiments at the battle were under strength.

Usually, the infantry battalions were tactically grouped into brigades comprising three or more battalions.

The British drill books not only described the minute detailing of the movements which the battalions must execute but also gave precise instructions as to how the men should march and how they would behave.

". . . The soldiers must carry their arms well and high, holding them firm on their shoulders and when they face to take care always to straighten their ranks and files . . ."

Much of Marlborough's success depended on his use and development of the platoon firing system which had been introduced into European warfare during the Thirty Years War. By this method, after the great column had wheeled into line and reduced itself into three ranks, it was divided off into platoons.

According to the size of the battalion the companies were sub-divided into 14-18 platoons each of an equal size, the grenadier company also being split, in the process, into two equal platoons and one despatched to each end of the battalion line.

Having been sub-divided into platoons, the Major of the battalion would then, in the words of the drill book ". . . tell them off into 'firings' usually of four to six platoons each".

Each 'firing' was arranged by the Major in random position in the line taking care that no two 'firings' were next to each other in the order of their sequence.

Having completed this arrangement the line of platoons was marched, with the Company Commanders two paces in front of their men, and with the Colonel or Lt. Colonel in the rear. When they reached about 60 yards from the enemy the line was halted and the ranks dressed. Then the Colonel, or Lt. Colonel, if he was in command, moved to the front in the centre of the line. The Colour Party moved into the centre behind the Colonel and two Drummers marched out to take post slightly behind him.

Each platoon was placed under the command of a Lieutenant with a sergeant deputed to maintain the dressings and order the firing. The Captains and the other officers and sergeants marched to the rear of the line and took up their posts, dressed their line and waited.

The first 'fire' usually consisted of 6 platoons, the second four platoons and the third a further four platoons.

When the battalion advanced, the officers were ordered to march two paces ahead of the men.

Orders were given either by word of mouth or by the drum. When the latter method was employed each order was preceded by what was known as a "preparative" which gave warning to the men that an instruction was to follow.

At each order the group of platoons whose 'firing' it was, made ready, and waited for their officers to give the necessary instructions to present and fire.

". . . The six platoons being the "first" fire make ready at once and take their firing from the right and left . . ."

Because the groups of platoons forming the various 'firings' had been scattered throughout the line the battalion commander could therefore bring an almost continual fire by volleys on his opponents.

It was usual for the whole battalion to fire a volley together after the separate platoon 'firings' had been executed and then the programme recommenced. A "street firing" technique was also employed which enabled a battalion fighting in the restricted confines of a built up area to bring continuous fire to bear on the enemy front. Each platoon fired to it's front, wheeled by half platoons and proceeded along the sides of the column of platoons to regain their position at the rear. The next platoon fired and they continued until resistance ceased. If they had to retreat they employed the same technique in reverse.

The drill books tried to cover every eventuality and had sections devoted to the intricate manoeuvres necessary in case of the battalion retreating; in the case of an enemy's sudden approach; attacking a battalion formed in line; how to "tell a battalion off to form a 'standing' square" and how to form a 'manoeuvring' square. All these movements entailed precise instructions so that they could all be reversed. Truly, they entailed what has been called "a choreography of war".

The commands for the handling of the musket included 42 orders and involved 161 different movements. Similarly, the grenadiers exercise for handling their cast iron bombs took a further 29 movements.

On parade, and when waiting orders to advance against an enemy, the officers stood with their half-pikes ordered. At the beat or 'flam' of the drum to call the battalion to order, officers and sergeants advanced their pikes and halberds. The orders were explicit, when that word of command was given or that 'flam' beat ". . . there must be a profound silence observed throughout the battalion and the soldiers must make no motion either of their feet, head, body or hands but such as is ordered, always keeping their eyes on the officer who is to give the order, carrying their firelocks straight on their shoulders, barrels straight up, muzzles steady, pressing the guard against their breasts, their feet a step distant, the heels in line and their toes turned out . . ."

ARTILLERY

The British Artillery was administered by the Board of Ordnance under the control of the Duke of Marlborough who held the post of Master-General of the Ordnance Branch in 1704. As such, their personnel had a somewhat privileged position and considered themselves superior to the cavalry and infantry. They were almost certainly better paid and equipped than the rest of the army and probably better clothed. Marlborough had the advantage of a ready formed artillery train when he decided to march on the Danube. He also had the advantage of having Colonel Holcroft Blood, a first class gunner and engineer to command it.

The great trains of artillery required a complicated heirarchy of specialists to keep the great variety of ordnance on the road and fit for battle. There was an enormous variety of ammunition, stores, tools and spares needed to keep the monster guns ready for action. Commanded by an officer known as the Train Controller it had an establishment which included Commissaries, a Paymaster, a Waggonmaster, a Quartermaster, a Provost Marshal, a Surgeon, a Farrier and his mates, a Master Gunner and his two mates, and officers who were known as Gentlemen of the Ordnance.

To maintain the great guns and their cumbersome carriages there were teams of carpenters, wheelwrights, collar and harness makers, coopers and artificers all needed to maintain the stock, tool and the quality of the shot and powder which had to be carried in innumerable waggons.

The guns were served by gunnery staff including Sergeants, Corporals and Mattrosses. The emplacements and fortified positions were prepared and maintained by a corps of Pioneers. There was also a special staff allocated the task of maintaining and manhandling the pontoon boats necessary to get the guns and the rest of the army over the countless rivers that had to be crossed. To protect the artillery trains there was a regiment known as the Regiment of Ordnance or Fusiliers later to become the 7th Royal Fusiliers. To lead the great column on the march there was a magnificently dressed kettledrummer who was mounted on a special horsedrawn waggon.

Some idea of the numbers of gunnery staff employed in Flanders in 1704 can be gauged from the Bills of Entries of the Ordnance Office now in the Public Record Office. This confirms that in 1703, 96 coats were required for the Sergeants, Corporals and Pontoon men and a further 70 for the Mattrosses and Pioneers.

The Guns

The guns were brass and mounted on wooden carriages. They consisted of a wide variety of sakers, howitzers, petards and mortars of varying sizes which included 36, 24, 18, 9, 6 and 3 pounders. In addition, each battalion of infantry had it's own two 3 pounder "galloper" guns mounted on special trailers and drawn by a single horse.

Field pieces were drawn by eight horses harnessed in tandem. Some of the heavier guns may have needed ten horses while the siege guns, 60, 48 and 38 pounder monster pieces, were drawn by an unlimited number of large horses harnessed in pairs.

The drivers were civilian peasants recruited for the campaign. They marched alongside the horses armed with long whips and, on some of the lighter guns, they may have ridden the horses.

The sergeant gunners were armed with halberds and hangers, the Corporals with partizans, the mattrosses with half-pikes and the gunners with linstocks. All had hangers worn on waist belts.

The pioneers carried a variety of tools including shovels, picks, adzes, mattocks and fascine and gabion knives. Their sergeants carried halberds and hangers.

Appendix 3

The French

CAVALRY

The French deployed their cavalry so that the regiment had a single troop front, massed up six ranks deep with a minimum distance between each rank. Their tactics involved trotting up, close to the enemy, then cantering to close quarters, the first rank discharging their pistols or carbines. Having done so they wheeled away by half troops right and left and wheeled back to the end of the column of squadrons where they took their places and re-loaded. The next rank then moved up in their turn and repeated the exercise. When the leading rank had worked their way through to the front again they repeated the action and then charged home with the sword to engage in a melee, often throwing their firearms at the enemy in the process.

This drill had been adequate when dealing with infantry armed with matchlock and pike or with cavalry who were only drilled to perform similar manoeuvres but had obvious shortcomings when confronted by cavalry such as Marlborough's which had been trained to charge with drawn swords and to whom the issue of ammunition had been deliberately restricted to ensure that their firearms were only used as protection when foraging.

Composition of the French Cavalry

In 1678 the French cavalry comprised four types of regiment. The Kings Household Troops ("Maison du Roi"), the Gentleman at Arms (" Gens d'armes "), The Light Cavalry ("Cavalerie Legers") and the Dragoons ("Les Dragoons") who, as in the British Army, were considered a quasi-infantry arm.

The Household Troops and the Gens d'armes were an élite force, richly dressed and equipped, and mounted on the largest and best black horses available. Louis XIV considered them to be invincible and treated the young nobility who clamoured to gain entry into the ranks as the cadre of officers who would eventually command other regiments as they matured.

There were 99 regiments of the so-called Light Cavalry of variable strength but usually consisting of four squadrons each of which had two troops of about 50 men.

Each troop was commanded by a Captain with long service with 1 Lieutenant and a "sous-lieutenant" (replacing the "Cornettes" in 1684). The troops had one "brigadier" for every ten troopers.

All the regiments had kettledrummers and there were two trumpeters and a standard allocated to each troop. The "cuirassiers du Roi" wore the complete cuirass, i.e. back and breast plate, the remainder wore the breast plate only and normally under the coat. Their hats were protected with an iron skull lining and some regiments still wore the old buff coats. Officers were armed with two pistols and a sabre and the men with sabre, carbine and two pistols. From 1691 two troopers of each troop were instructed in the use of, and were armed with, carbines and were eventually collated as an élite troop of "carabiniers" for each regiment. About 1700 the elite troops were re-formed as a regiment of "Carabiniers".

French line cavalry were split into two types, the regiments known as "De Grande Charges" or "Du Roi" which were either commanded by the King or other titular heads of the Royal Family. The others called "Regiments de Gentilhommes" which were known by the names of their Colonels, who were also the proprietors. In some contemporary documents they were referred to as "les Regiments Gris" apparently after the colour of their uniform coats.

INFANTRY

In the French infantry the battalion was larger than the British and is likely to have had as many as 1,000 men at full strength. They were also broken down into a company system each of which was the propriety of it's Captain ("Le propriete de son Capitaine"). The number of companies in a battalion varied in the French service and could be as low as ten or as high as twenty. In 1704 there were 251 regiments of French infantry some of which had as many as four battalions.

In 1661 the Commander of a regiment was known as "Mestre de Camp" but, mainly due to reforms introduced by the Duke of Opernon, the system was changed, and later the commanding officer became known as the Colonel. His staff comprised 1 Major and 1 Captain in charge of each company. The companies also included 1 lieutenant and a "Cornette".

Jean Martinet, whose name has become synonymous in the English language with a strict disciplinarian, is credited with the instruction that a company of grenadiers should be added to each infantry regiment. These élite troops were armed with an axe, sabre and a large pouch containing cartridges and grenades and a snap-hance musket.

The French infantry regiments carried three standards each of which had a white bow tied below the pike.

Mention has been made of the young conscript battalions which de Tallard used to reinforce de Marsin. Louvois had created what were known as the "milice provinciales" in France. A decree passed in 1688 laid down that every parish throughout the kingdom was obliged to provide and equip one militiaman between the ages of 24 and 40. The conscript served with the colours for two years. A recruiting poster of the period lists the ranks in a regiment of French infantry. These were 1 "Colonel", 1 "Lt. Colonel", 1 "Major", a "Capitaine" for each company, 1 "Lieutenant" for each company, 2 "Sous-Lieutenants" for each company, 1 "Ensign" for each company, and an unspecified number of "Sergents", "Caporaux", "Anspessades", "Grenadiere", "Mousquetaires", "Tambours", "Fifres" and "Vivandieres".

The old Colonel-General of Infantry, the Duc d'Erpernon, died in 1611 and the King himself assumed the post from that date, ably assisted by Francois Le Tellier, Marquis de Louvois. It was Louvois who appointed Generals Martinet and Fourille as the Inspecting Generals of the Cavalry and Infantry respectively and instituted the subsequent reforms throughout the French Army.

Martinet introduced volley firing into the French infantry and his system was still being used during the War of the Succession. The French infantry formed in line, five or six ranks deep, with the front rank kneeling, and fired by volleys one complete rank at a time. After the front rank had fired they had to crouch low or lie down to allow the rank behind to fire and they in turn had to either lie down or crouch over their comrades to allow the remainder to follow suit and re-load in turn. The inadequate system was considered a significant factor in the continuing success of Marlborough's armies.

THE ARTILLERY

The regiment of artillery proper was created in 1684 and titled the "Bombardiers Royale". There were two regiments each divided into twelve companies of gunners and one of miners. In 1693 a Regiment known as the "Fusiliers Royale" received the title "Regiment Royale D'Artillerie" and was thereafter employed solely to assist the artillery. By 1704 the French artillery comprised five battalions and together with the "Regiment Royale", totalled over 5,600 men.

The French artillery train employed non-military personnel to conduct it in the same manner as the British train. The guns were bronze and brass and their carriages painted blue.

Appendix 4
Biographical Notes

John Churchill, Duke of Marlborough (1650-1722)
Under Charles II he won much commendation and a peerage for his military services, and William III rewarded him with an earldom, but it was not until the War of the Spanish Succession that he attained full opportunity. Besides Blenheim which was the first major British victory over the French since Agincourt he added the splendid victories of Ramillies, Malplaquet and Oudenarde and was the most renowned general in Europe. The Queen granted him the estate at Woodstock and the beautiful Blenheim Palace which was designed by Vanbrugh. He also received a perpetual pension of £5,000 a year. In his later years Marlborough lost much of his popularity but George I restored him to some of his former glory when he made him Commander-in-Chief. On his death he was buried with great pomp in Westminster Abbey.

Francois Eugene, Prince of Savoy (1663-1736)
Born in Paris he was the son of Eugene Maurice, Count of Soissons and Olympia Mancini a niece of Cardinal Mazarin. Educated in France, he entered the Austrian Army because, it is said, Louis XIV refused to accept him in the French Army. He gained all his early experience against the Turks and made a great impression on all the military commanders who had contact with him. In 1691 he was fighting in Italy where he had several major successes over the French. In 1704 he began his collaboration with Marlborough. In 1706 he defeated the French at Turin and in 1708 fought at Oudenarde and later arranged the peace of Rastatt. Considered the greatest of all the soldiers who served Austria, Eugene had a passion for war but was also greatly interested in the arts. Said to have been a very ugly and hot tempered man.

General of Foot, Charles Churchill (1656-1714)

The third son of Sir Winston Churchill he joined the Duke of York's Maritime Regiment as an Ensign in the early 1670's and was promoted Captain in the Royal Dragoons in 1679. He became a Lt. Col. of the Tangier Regiment in 1682 and Colonel of the 3rd Foot in 1688. His promotion then was rapid, Major General in 1694; Lt. General 1702; General of Foot in September the same year and Colonel of the Coldstream Regiment in 1707.

General, John Lord Cutts (-1705)

Nicknamed the "Salamander" because of his incredible daring and bravery. He served for many years in the service of the United Provinces of the Netherlands and was the Colonel of a mercenary English Regiment of Foot in that service in 1688. Made Baron Cutts of Gowran, Co. Kilkenny in 1690, he became a Brigadier-General in 1693 and Colonel of the Coldstream Regiment in 1694. Promoted to Major-General in 1696 he became a Lt. General in 1703 and died two years after Blenheim.

George Hamilton, Lord Orkney (1666-1737)

The fifth son of the Duke of Hamilton he became a Captain in the Royal Regiment in 1684 and succeeded Colonel Lloyd as Colonel of the Inniskilling Regiment in 1690. Fought at the Boyne and at Aughrim. Colonel of the Ordnance Regiment in 1692 and the Royal Regiment in 1692. Created Earl of Orkney in 1696. Brigadier General in 1695, Major General 1702, Lt. General in 1704 and General of Foot in 1711. Governor of Virginia and of Edinburgh Castle and was made a Field Marshal in 1736. He died the following year.

William Earl of Cadogan (1675-1726)

Born in Dublin he entered the Army of William III as a Captain in Erle's Regiment in 1694 and became a Major in the Inniskillings in 1698. Appointed Quartermaster General in 1701 he served Marlborough in that capacity with great ability and was considered the best of his staff. He was appointed Colonel of the 5th Dragoon Guards in 1703, Brigadier-General in 1704; Colonel of the Coldstreams in 1714 and of the 1st Foot Guards in 1722. Created Baron Cadogan in 1716 and Earl in 1718. He was MP for Woodstock from 1705-16 and the British Minister in Holland from 1714-19. Buried in Westminster Abbey.

Camille D'Hostun, Comte de Tallard (also spelt Tallart) (1652-1728)

Appointed "Marechal de Camp" in 1688 he was promoted to Lt. General in 1693. Appointed Ambassador to London in 1698 and promoted Marshal of France in 1703. Taken prisoner at Blenheim he was sent to England where he lived for several years.

In 1712, after his return to France, he was made a Member of the Council of the Regency in 1717 and created Minister of State in 1726. De Tallard was elected to the Academy of Science in 1723 and died in 1728.

Maximillian Emanuel II von Wittelsbach, Elector of Bavaria (1662-1726)

Fought against the Turks from 1686-1688 and married Marie Antoinette, daughter of Leopold I of Austria (The Holy Roman Emperor) in 1685. Was made Governor of the Spanish Netherlands in 1691. His son Joseph Ferdinand was the hereditary heir to the throne of the King of Spain but died before Charles II. The Elector was a good, if unimaginative, soldier but after his defeat at Blenheim he retired into France.

Louis-William, Margrave of Baden (-1707)

Known as "Turken-Louis" he had gained a very good reputation fighting against the Turks. Baden was always treated with reserve by Marlborough who seems to have had doubts about his loyalty. After the Blenheim campaign he became unco-operative in his attitude towards Marlborough and Eugene because of slights offered to him during that campaign. He died in the Rhine sector in 1707 from blood poisoning.